The Ceilidh Dance Book

A Selection of the Most Popular Ceilidh Dances
With Step by Step Instructions and
Suggested Tune Sets

Selected and arranged by
Kevin Allison

Includes Standard and Open D Guitar Chords!

WWW. MELBAY. COM

Introduction

Thank you for purchasing

The Ceilidh Dance Book

A ceilidh (kay-leh) is a gathering together for people to share songs, stories, music and dancing. Assembling at a ceilidh was the way people traditionally socialised and entertained themselves. These days, a ceilidh event perhaps refers more to dancing than sharing songs and stories but it's a very important part of Scottish culture and remains a popular pastime.

This book introduces the most popular ceilidh dances with clear instructions for the dance steps and includes a selection of music that has been tried and tested to accompany the dances.

Demonstrations of most, if not all the dances in this book, can also be found on You Tube.

The dances in this book are introduced in order of a typical program that might be used at a ceilidh event, so it can be used as a guide.

Traditionally, each dance would be performed twice. There would be two rounds: the first time through to learn the dance, and a second time through to enjoy the dance. Each round might run through the dance four or five times.

The program in this book suggests the dances be performed once through, except for perhaps doing two "Gay Gordon's" at different times during the evening. The benefit of this means that timing-wise, you can introduce a greater variety of dances throughout the event. The program in this book presents twenty-four dances, but it is more likely that you will only dance through maybe a dozen or so, unless you keep dancing into the wee small hours.

The music introduced here for the dances, provides an effective guide for making up tune sets for ceilidh dancing! In Scotland, there are hundreds of ceilidh bands, each of which have their own sets of tunes so if you are familiar with other tune sets for the dances, then by all means use them. It is also not uncommon for the same tune to be used in different dances. An example would be "Farewell to the Dene". This tune is perhaps more familiar as a barn dance, but by changing the rhythm, it can also be used in a tune set for the "Gay Gordon's". Another tune used in this way is "Teribus", which I've placed in a barn dance setting, but it can also be used in a Gay Gordon's set.

I sincerely hope you enjoy this collection of ceilidh dances and music.

Thanks,
Kevin Allison

INDEX OF DANCES

Index of Tunes

Index of Tunes continued

Index of Tunes, continued

Bars	Gay Gordon's
	Formation: Couples form with gentleman's partner to his right, facing counterclockwise around the room.
1-2	Couples right hands joined over lady's right shoulder, gentleman's arm across lady's back, left hands joined in front. Starting on the right foot, walk forward for four steps.
3-4	While walking in the same direction - counterclockwise, and still holding your partner, pivot on the spot so that the gentleman's left arm is behind the lady to join left hands over Lady's left shoulder, and right hands are joined at the front. Continue walking backwards for another four steps.
5-8	Repeat previous steps in the opposite direction, clockwise round the room.
9-12	Drop hands, gentleman raises right hand above lady's head. Lady's right hand joins gent's right hand, then lady pivots and turns round underneath gent's right hand four times. (As the Lady pivots and turns, gents take four small steps counterclockwise to follow his partner.)
13-16	Gentleman takes his partner in ballroom hold, and both polka (spin) counterclockwise around the room to finish the dance, ready to start again. Repeat dance as many times as you want.

TUNE SET:

Jerry Hayes...p. 8
Campbell's Farewell to Redcastle Key G...p. 8
Campbell's Farewell to Redcastle Key A...p. 9
Farewell to the Dene...p. 9

Jerry Hayes

Reel played as March tempo

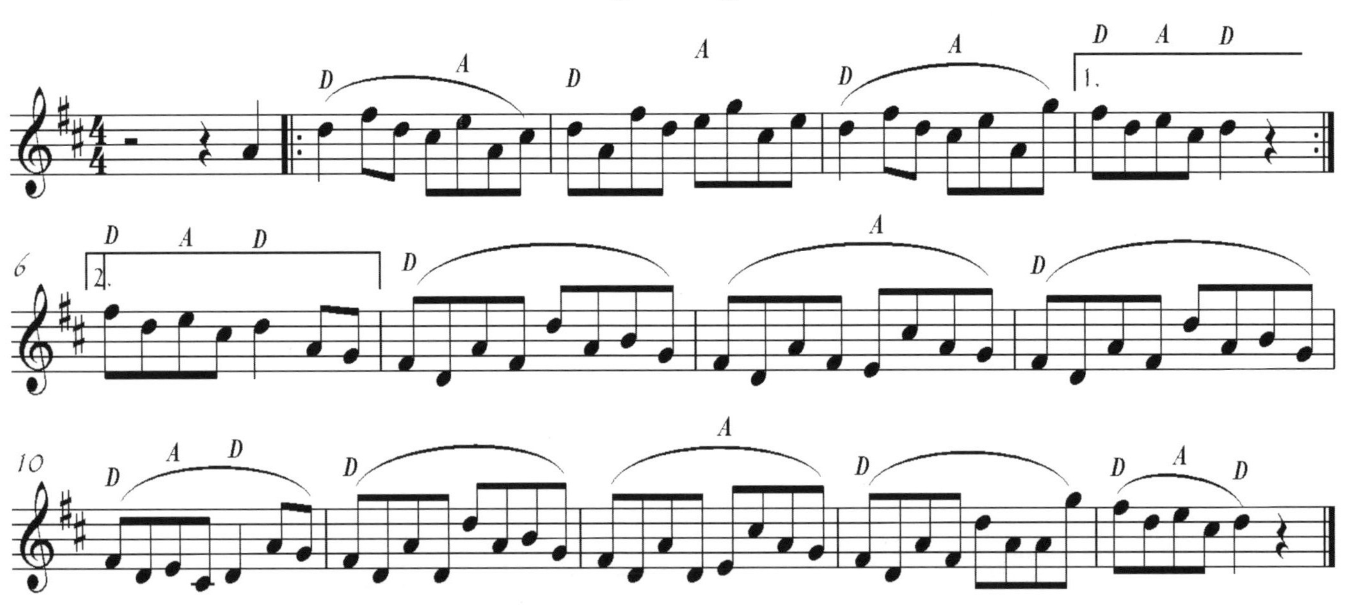

Campbell's Farewell to Redcastle

Traditional

Campbell's Farewell to Redcastle

Traditional

Bars	Canadian Barn Dance
	Formation: Couples form with gentleman's partner to his right-hand side facing counterclockwise around the room.
1-2	Lead off with the outside foot and walk forward for three steps, then hop.
3-4	Walk backwards for three steps, then hop.
5-6	Take two steps sideways away from your partner (men stepping to the center of the room, ladies stepping to the edge of the room) and clap your hands.
7-8	Return to your partner and adopt the ballroom or waltz hold.
9-12	Gentlemen lead their partners two sidesteps to the gentleman's left (lady's right) then back again.
13-16	Gentlemen lead their partners to polka (spin) around counterclockwise to finish the dance, ready to start again. Repeat dance as many times as you want.

TUNE SET:

The Colosseum

Traditional

John McAlpine's
Traditional
A D A E A D A E A
6
A D A E A D A E A
Teribus
Traditional
D Bm Em A D Bm G A D
10
D Bm Em A D Bm G A D
18
D Bm Em A D Bm G A D

Bars	St Bernards Waltz
	Formation: Couples form with gentlemen taking their partners in waltz hold, ladies facing the center of the room, dancing counterclockwise.
1-4	Gentlemen lead their partners and take three sidesteps left counterclockwise around the room; close feet with a stamp.
5-6	Gentlemen lead their partners and take two steps to the right (clockwise).
7-8	Gentlemen lead their partners and take two steps back towards the center of the room. (Ladies move forward with right foot, then left foot; gentlemen move back with left foot then right foot.)
9-10	Gentlemen lead their partners and take two steps forward, back out again.
11-12	gentlemen raise their right hands above their partner's head. Lady's right hand joins gent's right hand and lady pivots on the spot, turning beneath gent's right hand.
13-16	Gentlemen lead their partners and waltz counterclockwise around the room to finish the dance, ready to start again. Repeat dance as many times as you want.

TUNE SET:

Bonnie Galawa...p. 14
My Wee Laddie...p. 14
Westering Home...p. 15

Bonnie Galawa
Traditiona
G D C G G Em Am
D G D C G G Em D G
G Em C G G Em Am D
G D C G G Em D G
My Wee Laddie
Traditional
C D G Em Am D G
C D G Em Am D G
G C G Em Am D
G C
D G

Westering Home

Traditional

Bars	Boston Two Step
	Formation: Couples form side by side, holding hands with gentleman's partner on right, dancing counterclockwise around the room.
1-2	While holding hands, both gentlemen and ladies take a pas de basque step, (step right and close feet, then step left and close feet) away from each other then step back together again.
3-4	Gentlemen lead their partners and take three steps forward (counterclockwise) and turn.
5-6	While holding hands, both gentlemen and ladies take another pas de basque step away from each other, then step back together again.
7-8	Gentlemen lead their partners and take three steps forward (clockwise), turn and face partners.
9	Holding both hands together, both gentlemen and ladies jump, and kick right foot across front of partner to left.
10	Holding both hands together, both gentlemen and ladies jump, and kick left foot across front of partner to right.
11-12	Gentleman then offers his right hand above lady's head, then lady joins right hands and turns once under the gentleman's arm.
13-16	Gentlemen then lead their partners to polka (spin) round counterclockwise to finish the dance ready to start again. Repeat dance as many times as you want.

TUNE SET:

Sarah's Jig...p. 17
Lady in the House...p. 17
Drummond Castle...p. 18
The Rising River ...p. 18

Sarah's Jig
Kevin Allison
Lady in the House
Kevin Allison

Drummond Castle
Traditional
The Rising River
Kevin Allison

Bars	The Dashing White Sergeant
	Formation: Sets of three facing three to make up a set of six – either one gentleman and two ladies to make up a set of three, or one lady and two gentlemen. This dance requires at least four or five sets of six to work properly.
1-8	In your set of six, join hands in a circle and dance round to the left (clockwise) for eight steps, then dance back round to the right (counterclockwise) for eight steps.
9-12	Drop hands, and in your set of three, the person in the middle turns (sets) to the partner on their right. Each then takes a pas de basque step, (step right and close feet, then step left and close feet) then turn your partner once round by the right hand (you can also use both hands).
13-16	The person in the middle then turns (sets) to their partner on their left, repeats the pas de basque step, then turns their partner once round as before.
17-24	The person in the middle then sets once again to their partner on the right. The person swings their partner round by the right arm then does the same with their other partner by the left arm. Repeat these steps again to finish up in your set of three again. (This is known as the figure of eight pattern.)
25-28	Join hands in your set of three, then advance for four steps towards the set of three facing you and then retire.
29-32	Both sets of three advance again towards each other. This time, one set raises their arms and the other set moves forward under the set who have raised their arms. Each set of three will then have a new set facing them to start the dance again.

TUNE SET:

The Dashing White Sergeant

Traditional

The Rose Tree
Traditional
D
G A
D A
D
G A
9
D
1.
D
2.
D
Em
A
15
D
G A
D
1.
D
2.
Miss McLeod's Reel
Traditional
A
Bm E
A
7
D
A E
A
12
A
Bm E
A
16
D
A E
1.
A E
2.

Willajford
Traditional
The High Road to Linton
Traditional

Bars	Scottish Waltz
	Formation: Gentlemen take their partners in ballroom (waltz) hold. There are no set dance steps for this so you can just waltz with your partner around the room. I've put it in the program here to give folks a rest after dancing "The Dashing White Sergeant", which is a fairly long and fast dance.

TUNE SET:

Soraidh...p. 23
River Waltz...p. 24

Soraidh

Traditional

The River Waltz

Kevin Allison

Bars	Haymaker's Jig
	Formation: Sets of four couples in rows, gentlemen facing their partners with their left shoulder towards the band (top of the room).
1-4	First lady (Couple no 1) and last gentleman (Couple no 4) advance to the center of the set, offer right hands to each other, turn once round, then retire to places.
5-8	First gentleman (Couple no 1) and last lady (Couple no 4) advance to center of the set, offer right hands to each other, turn once round, then retire to places.
9-12	First lady (Couple no 1) and last gentleman (Couple no 4) advance to center of the set, offer left hands to each other, turn once round, then retire to places.
13-16	First gentleman (Couple no 1) and last lady (Couple no 4) advance to center of the set, offer left hands to each other, turn once round, then retire to places.
17-20	First lady (Couple no 1) and last gentleman (Couple no 4) advance to center of the set, offer both hands to each other, turn once round, then retire to places.
21-24	First gentleman (Couple no 1) and last lady (Couple no 4) advance to center of the set, offer both hands to each other, turn once round, then retire to places.
25-28	First lady (Couple no 1) and last gentleman (Couple no 4) advance to center of the set, pass round each other back to back (do si do), then retire to places.
29-32	First gentleman (Couple no 1) and last lady (Couple no 4) advance to center of the set, pass round each other back to back (do si do), then retire to places.

Bars	Haymaker's Jig - Continued
33-36	First lady (Couple no 1) and last gentleman (Couple no 4) advance to center of the set, curtsey and bow to say, "Thank you for dancing with me", then retire to places.
37-40	First gentleman (Couple no 1) and last lady (Couple no 4) advance to center of the set, curtsey and bow to say, "thank you for dancing with me", then retire to places.
41-48	First couple join hands and dance down to the bottom of the set, then split (cast off) so that the first lady leads all the ladies back up the outside of the set to the top. The first gentleman will likewise lead all the gentlemen back up the outside of the set to the top. The first couple then join hands above their heads and all the other couples pass underneath to form the set once again. This part of the Dance is just like the "Grand Old Duke of York dance."

TUNE SET:

Wellington's Advance...p. 27
Charlie Stewart...p. 27
The Humors of Glendart...p. 28
Hartigan's Fancy ...p. 28

Wellington's Advance

The Humors of Glendart

Traditional

Bars	Pride of Erin Waltz
	Formation: Couples side by side, gentlemen with their partners to their right, facing counterclockwise around the room. (This is perhaps one of the more difficult dances to explain, so please take your time to read the instructions carefully.)
1-4	Gentleman offers right hand to lady, lady takes gentleman's right hand with her left hand. Gentleman swings right leg forward and back, lady swings left leg forward and back. Gentleman leads lady forward for three steps, and they turn to face each other.
5-8	Gentleman offers left hand to lady, lady takes gentleman's left hand with her right hand. Gentleman swings left leg forward and back, lady swings right leg forward and back. Gentleman leads lady forward for three steps, then they turn to face each other.
9-10	Facing your partner, couples join hands. Gentlemen leading counterclockwise, cross right foot across left foot then point left foot to lead. (Lady crosses left foot across right foot then points right foot to lead.)
11-12	Gentlemen leading clockwise, cross left foot across right foot then point right foot to lead. (Lady crosses right foot across left foot, then point left foot to lead.)
13-16	Couples facing each other, gentlemen join right hand with ladies' left hand and move counterclockwise, swinging away from each other. (Gentleman's left shoulder swings half turn away from lady, and lady's right shoulder swings half turn, away from gentleman x 2.) (Swing out, swing in, swing out, swing in = 4 steps.)
17-24	Couples facing each other, joining both hands. Swing forward towards each other, (Slightly to the side of your partner) swing back away from each other. Swing forward again and this time, while holding hands, couples cross over/under gentlemen's left arm (swapping places) and turn. Repeat swings and step back to original places.
25-28	Couple in ballroom hold. Gentlemen lead their partners two steps left (counterclockwise), then two steps right (clockwise).
29-32	Couples waltz around the room counterclockwise to finish the dance and take up positions, ready to start again. Repeat dance as many times times as you want.

TUNE SET:

When Irish Eyes Are Smiling...p. 30

The Rose of Aranmore...p. 30

Rosin the Bow...p. 31

When Irish Eyes Are Smiling
Traditional
The Rose of Aranmore
Traditional

Rosin the Bow

Traditional

Bars	Strip the Willow
	Formation: Sets of four couples in rows, gentlemen facing their partners with their left shoulder towards the band (top of the room).
1-8	First couple nearest the band, join hands and spin round for the count of 16 beats.
9-16	First lady then turns second gentleman by right hand, then turns their partner by left hand. First lady then turns third gentleman by right hand, then turns their partner by left hand. First lady then turns fourth gentleman by right hand, then turns their partner by left hand.
17-24	First couple should now be at the bottom of the set! First couple join hands and spin round for the count of 8 beats.
25-32	First gentleman then turns fourth lady by right hand, then turns their partner by left hand. First gentleman then turns third lady by right hand, then turns their partner by left hand. First gentleman then turns second lady by right hand, then turns their partner by left hand.
33-40	First couple should now be at the top of the set! First couple join hands and spin round for the count of 8 beats.
41-48	At the same time, first lady turns second gentleman and first gentleman turns second lady. First lady and first gentleman turn each other and continue turning couple three and four in this way to the bottom of the set.
49-56	First couple join hands and spin round for the count of 8 beats to finish the dance. The second couple who are now at the top of the set, lead off to start the next round of the dance.

TUNE SET:

The Banks of the Allan...p. 33

Atholl Highlanders...p. 33

Shandon Bells...p. 34

Stool of Repentance...p. 34

Yellow John...p. 35

Note: After playing "Yellow John", you might consider finishing the set off with "Atholl Highlanders" again, and perhaps play the tune really fast!

The Banks of the Allan

Traditional

Atholl Highlanders

Traditional

Shandon Bells

Traditional

Yellow John

Traditional

Bars	Gay Gordon's
	Formation: Couples form with gentleman's partner to his right, facing counterclockwise around the room.
1-2	Couples join right hands over lady's right shoulder with gentleman's arm across lady's back, and left hands joined in front. Starting on the right foot, walk forward for four steps.
3-4	While walking in the same direction - counterclockwise, and still holding your partner, pivot on the spot so that the gentleman's left arm is behind the lady to join left hands over Lady's left shoulder, and right hands are joined at the front. Continue walking backwards for another four steps.
5-8	Repeat previous steps in the opposite direction, clockwise round the room.
9-12	Drop hands, gentleman raises right hand above lady's head. Lady's right hand joins gent's right hand, then lady pivots and turns round underneath gent's right hand four times. (As the lady pivots and turns, gents take four small steps counterclockwise to follow his partner.)
13-16	Gentleman takes his partner in ballroom hold, and both polka (spin) counterclockwise around the room to finish the dance, ready to start again. Repeat dance as many times as you want.

TUNE SET 2:

Scotland the Brave
Traditional
Dornoch Links
Traditional

The Barren Rocks of Aden

Traditional

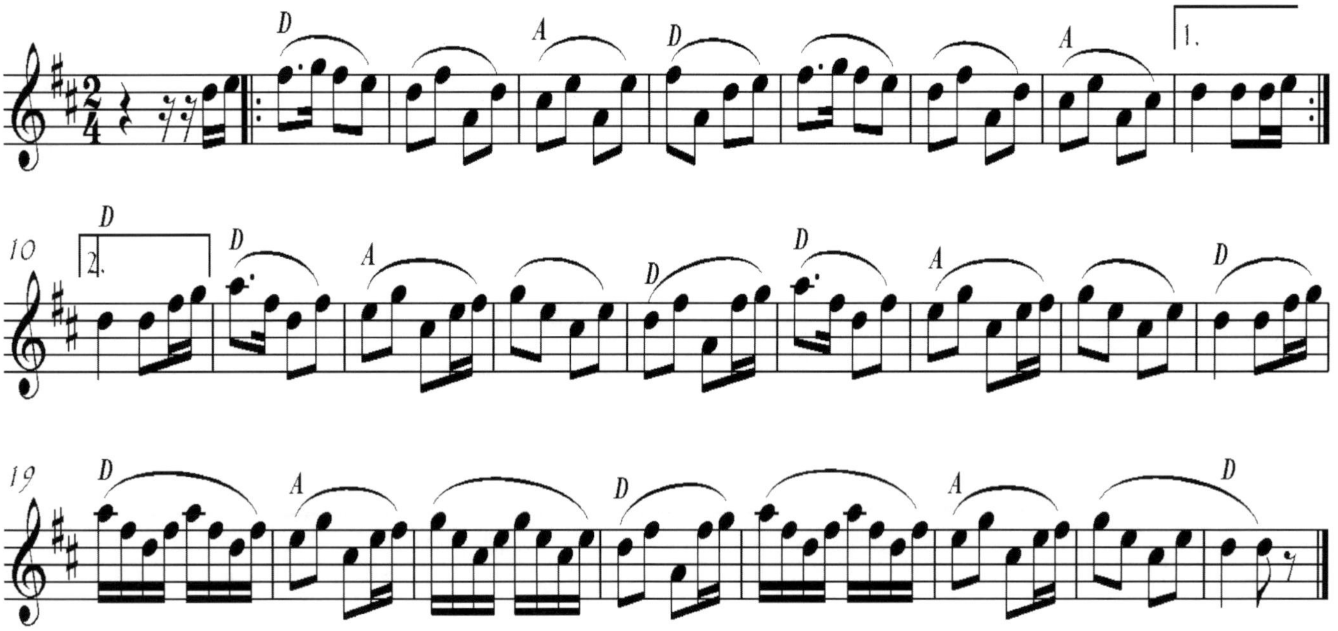

Bars	St Bernards Waltz
	Formation: Couples form with gentleman taking his partner in waltz hold, lady facing the center of the room, dancing counterclockwise.
1-4	Gentlemen lead their partners and take three sidesteps left (counterclockwise around the room), close feet with a stamp.
5-6	Gentlemen lead their partners and take two steps to the right (clockwise).
7-8	Gentlemen lead their partners and take two steps back towards the center of the room. (Ladies move forward with right foot then left foot, gentlemen move back with left foot then right foot.)
9-10	Gentlemen lead their partners and take two steps forward, back out again.
11-12	gentlemen raise their right hands above their partner's head. Lady's right hand joins gent's right hand and lady pivots on the spot, turning beneath gent's right hand.
13-16	Gentlemen lead their partners and waltz counterclockwise around the room to finish the dance, ready to start again. Repeat dance as many times as you want.

TUNE SET 2:

Glencoe...p. 40

Leezie Lindsay...p. 40

Ye Banks and Braes...p. 41

Glencoe
Traditional
Leezie Lindsay
Traditional

Ye Banks and Braes

Traditional

Bars	Virginia Reel
	Formation: Sets of four couples in rows, gentlemen facing their partners with their left shoulder towards the band (top of the room).
1-8	All couples advance towards their partners for three steps then on the fourth step, stamp their feet and clap hands, then retire to places.
9-16	Repeat steps as before.
17-24	All couples advance towards each other and turn each other by the right arm, then retire to places.
25-32	All couples advance towards each other and turn each other by the left arm, then return to places.
33-40	All couples advance towards each other and turn each other with both arms, then retire to places.
41-48	All couples advance towards each other and pass each other back to back, left shoulder by left shoulder (do-si-do), then retire to places.
49-56	First couple at the top of the set, join hands and dance down to the bottom of the set and back up again.
57-64	First couple then splits (casts off) so that the first lady leads all the ladies down the outside of the set to the bottom. The first gentleman will likewise lead all the gentlemen down the outside of the set to the bottom. The first couple then join hands above their heads and all the other couples pass under the first couple back up to form the set once again. Repeat dance as many times as you want.

TUNE SET :

Jaybird...p. 43
The Turkey in the Straw...p. 43
Oh Suzannah...p. 44
Arkansas Traveler...p. 44

Jaybird

Traditional

The Turkey in the Straw

Traditional

Oh Susannah

Traditional

Arkansas Traveler

Traditional

Bars	Brittania Two Step
	Formation: Sets of three, either one man and two ladies, or one lady and two gentlemen. Side by side, hands joined, facing counterclockwise around the room.
1-2	Starting with left foot, heel to the floor, toe to the floor, take two steps forward to the left.
3-4	Heel to the floor, toe to the floor, step forward to the right. (two steps)
5-8	Set moves forward for three steps; hop, then take three steps back.
9-12	Partners set to facing forward (counterclockwise) and all partners take a pas de basque step (step right and close feet, then step left and close feet). The person in the middle then does another pas de basque step while raising their arms above, for both partners to turn underneath.
13-16	Set moves forward for three steps; hop, then three steps back. Repeat the dance as many times as you want

TUNE SET :

The Highlander Jig...p. 46
The Bugle Horn...p. 46
Banjo Breakdown...p. 47

The Highlander Jig

Traditional

The Bugle Horn

Traditional

Banjo Breakdown

Traditional

Bars	**Canadian Barn Dance – Progressive**
	Formation: Couples form with gentleman's partner to his right-hand side, facing counterclockwise around the room.
1-2	Lead off with the outside foot and walk forward for three steps, then hop.
3-4	Walk backwards for three steps, then hop.
5-6	Take two steps sideways away from your partner (men stepping to the center of the room, ladies stepping to the edge of the room) and clap your hands.
7-8	(Progressive section) As the gentleman returns from the center of the room, his original partner moves forward to meet up with the next gentleman. The gentleman then takes up his position, with the next lady moving forward to meet him. At this point, each time through the dance, everyone will have changed partners. This is a really good way to get people to mix.
9-12	Gentlemen lead their partners two sidesteps to the gentleman's left (lady's right), then back again.
13-16	Gentlemen lead their partners to polka (spin) around counterclockwise to finish the dance, ready to start again. Repeat dance as many times as you want.

TUNE SET 2:

Bantry Bay...p. 49
The Honeysuckle...p. 49
Ballincollig in the Morning...p. 50

Bantry Bay

Traditional

The Honeysuckle

Traditional

Ballincollig in the Morning

Traditional

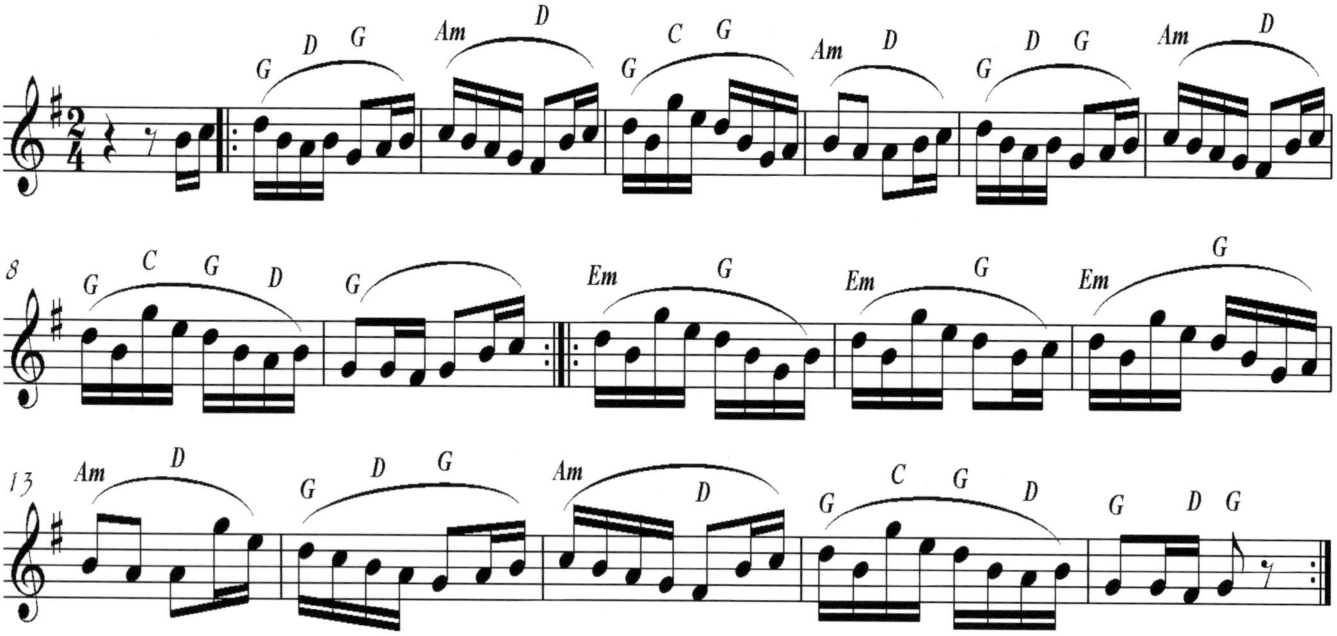

Bars	Scottish Waltz
	Formation: Gentlemen take their partner in ballroom (waltz) hold. There are no set dance steps for this so you can just waltz with your partner around the room.

TUNE SET 2:

Sine Bhan

Kisimul's Galley

Traditional

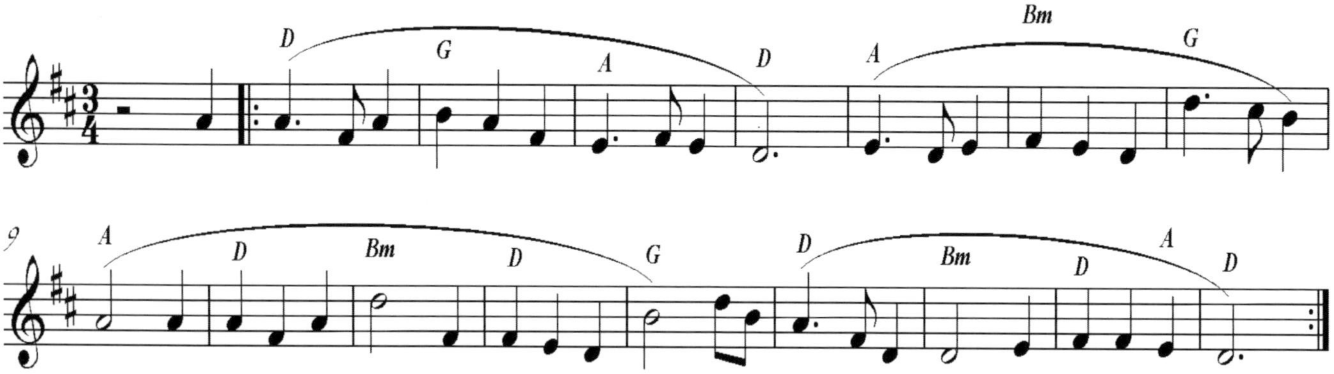

The Song of Home

Traditional

Bars	Circassian Circle
	Formation; Couples form with gentleman's partner to his right and couples joining hands in a big circle round the room.
1-4	All couples dance round to the left (clockwise) for eight steps, then dance round to the right (counterclockwise) for eight steps.
5-8	All couples advance to the center for four steps, then retire for four steps.
9-12	Everyone drop hands, then just the ladies join hands and advance four steps to the center, clap their hands, then retire.
13-16	Gentlemen then join hands and advance four steps to the center, clap their hands, then retire.
17-20	Couples turn and set to (face) your partner. Turn (spin) your partner round once.
21-32	Couples form in promenade hold. (Side by side - gentleman's right hand takes lady's right hand and gentleman's left hand takes lady's left hand.) Dance counterclockwise around the room to finish the dance. Repfat the dance as many times as you want.

TUNE SET:

Roxburgh Castle...p. 54

Soldier's Joy...p. 54

The Rakes of Mallow...p. 55

The Jolly Beggarman...p. 55

Roxburgh Castle

Rakes of Mallow

Traditional

Bars	American Circle Dance (Progressive)
	Formation: Couples form side by side, gentlemen facing counterclockwise, ladies facing clockwise, joining right hands at elbow or shoulder height.
1-4	Couples start; stamp their right feet twice, then cross over in front of each other for two steps, then join left hands and stamp their left feet twice.
5-8	Couples cross over again in front of each other for two steps, then repeat steps as before.
9-12	Couples then turn each other by the right hand once round, back to your starting positions.
13-16	At the same time, both partners advance (dance) round the room for four steps. Gentlemen move counterclockwise, ladies move clockwise to meet up with new partners, ready to start the dance again.

TUNE SET:

Arran Air…p. 57
The Girl I left Behind Me…p. 57
The Forty-Two Pound Float…p. 58
Farewell to Whiskey…p. 58

Arran Air
Traditional
The Girl I Left Behind Me
Traditional

The Forty Two Pound Float

Traditional

Farewell to Whiskey

Traditional

Bars	Cumberland Square Eight
	Formation: Sets of four couples set out in a square formation; gentlemen with their partner to their right. Couple Number One with their backs to the band top of the room (12 O'clock), Couple Number Two at 3 O'clock, Couple Number Three at 6 O'clock, Couple Number Four at 9 O'clock. (Couples One and Three facing each other, and Couples Two and Four facing each other.)
1-8	Couples One and Three taking waltz hold with their partners, dance across the set, dance round each other by the gentlemen's right shoulder, then dance back to places.
9-16	Couples Two and Four repeat the previous steps.
17-24	Couples One and Three advance to the center and dance a right-hand star (join right hands and circle right) for four steps, then dance left-hand star (join left hands and circle left) for four steps.
25-32	Couples Two and Four repeat the previous steps.
33-40	Couples One and Three advance to the centre and form a `basket`, which means to form a circle with the gentlemen joining hands behind the ladies backs, ladies arms rest on the gentlemen's arms. Circle to the left for eight steps to get back to your original places. (If you swing round fast enough, the ladies will be able to lift their feet off the ground.)
41-48	Couples Two and Four repeat the previous steps.
49-56	All couples join hands and circle to the left for eight steps, then circle to the right for eight steps. (Note: You can alternatively, circle to the left for sixteen steps.)
57-64	Couples then form in promenade hold (side by side - gentleman's right hand takes lady's right hand and gentleman's left hand takes lady's left hand). Dance counterclockwise around the room to finish the dance. Repeat the dance as many times as you want.

TUNE SET :

Molly What Ails You?

Traditional

The Wind that shakes the Barley

Traditional

Bars	Eva 3 Step
	Formation: Couples form side by side facing counterclockwise around the room with gentleman's partner to his right holding hands at shoulder height. (or at whatever height is comfortable)
1-2	Couples advance forward for three steps, then close feet together. (Count 4)
3-4	Walk three steps sideways crossing over each other. Gentleman steps across behind lady and lady steps across in front of the gentleman, (swapping places) then clap hands. (Count 4)
5-6	Walk three steps sideways, crossing over each other again. Gentleman steps across in front of the lady, and the lady steps across behind the gentleman, back to their original places. (Count 4)
7-8	Couples join hands again and walk backwards (clockwise) for three steps.
9-12	Couples step slightly forward away from each other, turning back to back once round to face their partners again.
13-16	Gentlemen then set (step) with your partner to the left then right, then waltz to finish the dance. Repeat the dance as many times as you want.

TUNE SET:

St Lawrence Jig...p. 63
Farewell to the Tay...p. 63
The Rising River II...p. 64

St Lawrence Jig

Traditional

Farewell to the Tay

Traditional

The Rising River II

Kevin Allison

Bars	Highland Scottishe
	Formation: Couples form facing each other, adopting the ballroom hold, gentlemen with their backs to the center of the room, Dancing counterclockwise around the room.
1-2	Gentleman with left foot, lady with right foot, point toe, then bring foot up with heel to front of shin of the other leg. Point toe again, and bring foot up behind the calf of the other leg.
3-4	Step onto pointing foot, again close feet; take another step onto pointing foot and close feet.
5-8	Repeat bars 1-2 and 3-4 with opposite feet - Gentlemen, repeat with right foot pointing and ladies with left foot pointing.
9-12	Gentlemen lead their partners to step and close, step and close to the left. Then to step and close, step and close to the right.
13-16	Gentlemen lead their partners to polka (spin round) counterclockwise around the room to finish the dance. Repeat the dance as many times as you want.

TUNE SET:

The Orange and Blue...p. 66
The Keel Row...p. 66

The Orange and Blue

Traditional

The Keel Row

Traditional

Bars	Lomond Waltz
	Formation: Couples form facing each other adopting the ballroom hold, gentlemen with their backs to the center of the room. (Dancing counterclockwise around the room.)
1-8	Gentlemen lead their partners two steps to the left, then two steps back towards the center of the room, two steps to the right, then two steps forward back to their original places.
9-12	Couples turn away from each other back to back, join hands, then continue round to face their partners again (one complete turn).
13-16	Couples facing each other, joining both hands. Swing forward towards each other, (slightly to the side of your partner), then swing back away from each other. Swing forward again, and this time, while holding hands, couples cross over, under gentlemen's left arm (swapping places) and turn.
17-20	Repeat swings and steps back to original places. (Gentleman's backs to the center of the room.)
21-24	Gentlemen lead their partners; step to the left and cross right foot over left foot, then point left foot. (Ladies will step to the right and cross left foot over right foot then point right foot.)
25-28	Gentlemen lead their partners in opposite direction, step to the right and cross left foot over right foot then point right foot. (Ladies will step to the left and cross right foot over left foot, then point left foot.)
29-32	Gentlemen lead their partners to waltz counterclockwise round the room. Repeat the dance as many times as you want.

TUNE SET:

Tuireadh Iain Ruaidh...p. 68

Welcome to Skye...p. 68

South Georgia Whaling Song...p. 69

Tuireadh Iain Ruaidh
Traditional
Welcome to Skye
Traditional

South Georgia Whaling Song

Traditional

Bars	Orcadian Strip the Willow (Shetland Reel)
	Formation: couples form in rows, Gentlemen facing their partners with their left shoulder towards the band (top of the room). A minimum of eight couples for this dance is required, but if you can get up to sixteen couples, that would be better!
1-8	First couple at the top of the set, nearest the band, join hands and spin round for the count of 16 beats.
9 -	At the same time, first lady then turns the second gentleman and first gentleman turns the second lady. First lady and first gentleman then turn each other, and then continue turning all the other couples in the same way dancing down to the bottom of the set.
...	First couple should now be at the bottom of the set to join the line of couples. Each new couple at the top of the set will start the dance after every 16 bars of music or when the couple before them have danced (spun round) down two couples in the set. (Please note the absence of bar numbers! The number of bars of music for this section will depend on the number of couples on the dance floor. In other words, it will take longer for each couple to dance down a set of twelve couples than a set of eight couples.)
...	New first couple now at the top of the set, join hands, and spin round for the count of 16 beats.
...	New first couple then work (dance) their way down the set in the same way as the previous couple.
...	Repeat the previous steps for each couple in the set. With each couple starting the dance after every 16 bars, you will effectively end up with the whole line of couples swinging each other continuously which makes the dance great fun to do especially if the music is played fast.

TUNE SET:

The Hills of Glenorchy...p. 71
The Mooncoin Jig...p. 71
Tim the Thatcher...p. 72
The Humors of Cappa...p. 72

You can also change from Jigs to Reels during this dance
to make it more interesting.

The Hills of Glenorchy

Traditional

Tim the Thatcher
Traditional
The Humors of Cappa
Traditional

Bars	Military Two Step
	Formation: Couples form side by side, with gentlemen holding hands with partner on right, dancing counterclockwise around the room.
1-2	Couples heel, toe, heel, toe. (Gentlemen heel toe with left foot, ladies heel toe with right foot.)
3-4	Gentlemen lead their partners and take three steps forward (counterclockwise) and turn.
5-6	Couples heel, toe, heel, toe. (Gentlemen heel toe with right foot, ladies heel toe with left foot.)
7-8	Gentlemen lead their partners and take three steps forward (clockwise) and turn to face partners.
9	Holding both hands together, both gentlemen and ladies jump, and kick right foot across front of partner to left.
10	Holding both hands together, both gentlemen and ladies jump, and kick left foot across front of partner to right.
11-12	Gentleman offers right hand above lady's head, then lady joins right hands and turns once round under gentleman's arm.
13-16	Gentlemen lead their partners to polka (spin) round counterclockwise to finish the dance, ready to start again. Repeat dance as many times as you want.

TUNE SET:

Cock o' the North

Traditional

Smash the Windows

Traditional

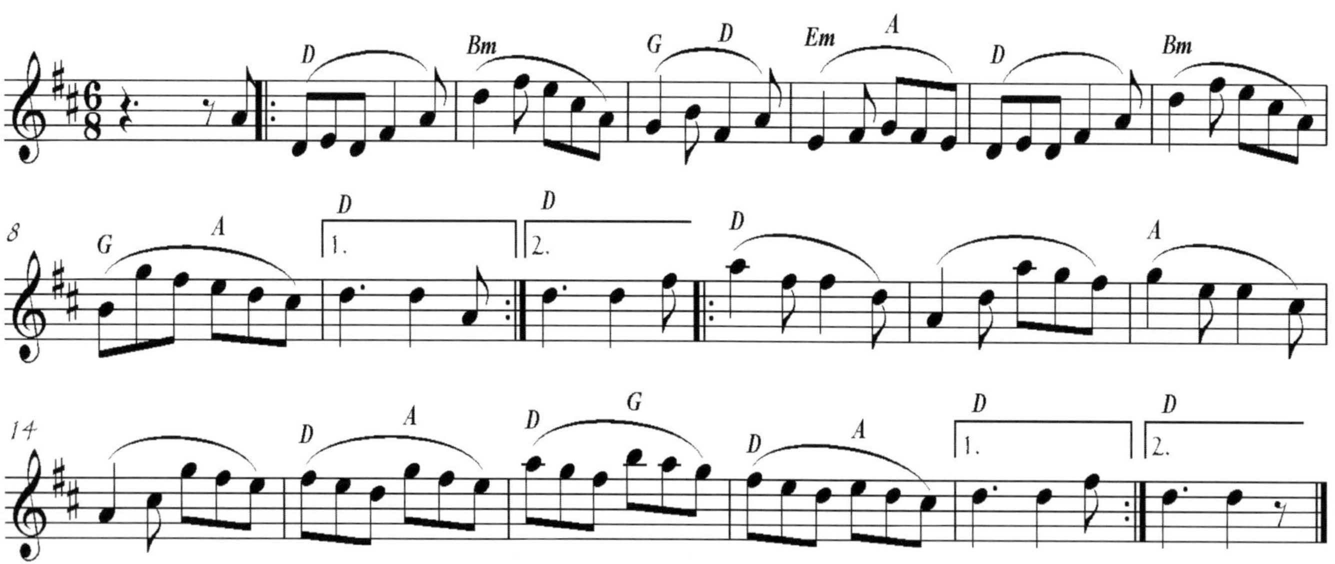

The Devil in Dublin

Traditional

Bars	Gay Gordon's
	Formation: Couples form with gentleman's partner to his right, facing counterclockwise around the room.
1-2	Couples join right hands over lady's right shoulder, with gentleman's arm across lady's back and left hands joined in front. Starting on the right foot, walk forward four steps.
3-4	While walking in the same direction - (counterclockwise) and still holding your partner, pivot on the spot so that the gentleman's left arm is behind the lady, and left hands are joined over the lady's left shoulder, and right hands are joined at the front. Continue walking backwards for another four steps.
5-8	Repeat previous steps in the opposite direction, clockwise round the room.
9-12	Drop hands, gentleman raises right hand above lady's head. Lady's right hand joins gent's right hand, then lady pivots and turns round underneath gent's right hand four times. (As the Lady pivots and turns, gents take four small steps counterclockwise to follow their partners.)
13-16	Gentleman takes his partner in ballroom hold, and both polka (spin) counterclockwise around the room to finish the dance, ready to start again. Repeat dance as many times as you want.

TUNE SET 3:

The Earl of Mansfield...p. 77
The Sweet Maid of Glendaurel...p. 77
Lady McKenzie of Coull...p. 78
The 72nd Highlander's Farewell to Edinburgh...p. 78

The Earl of Mansfield

Traditional

Lady McKenzie of Coull

Traditional

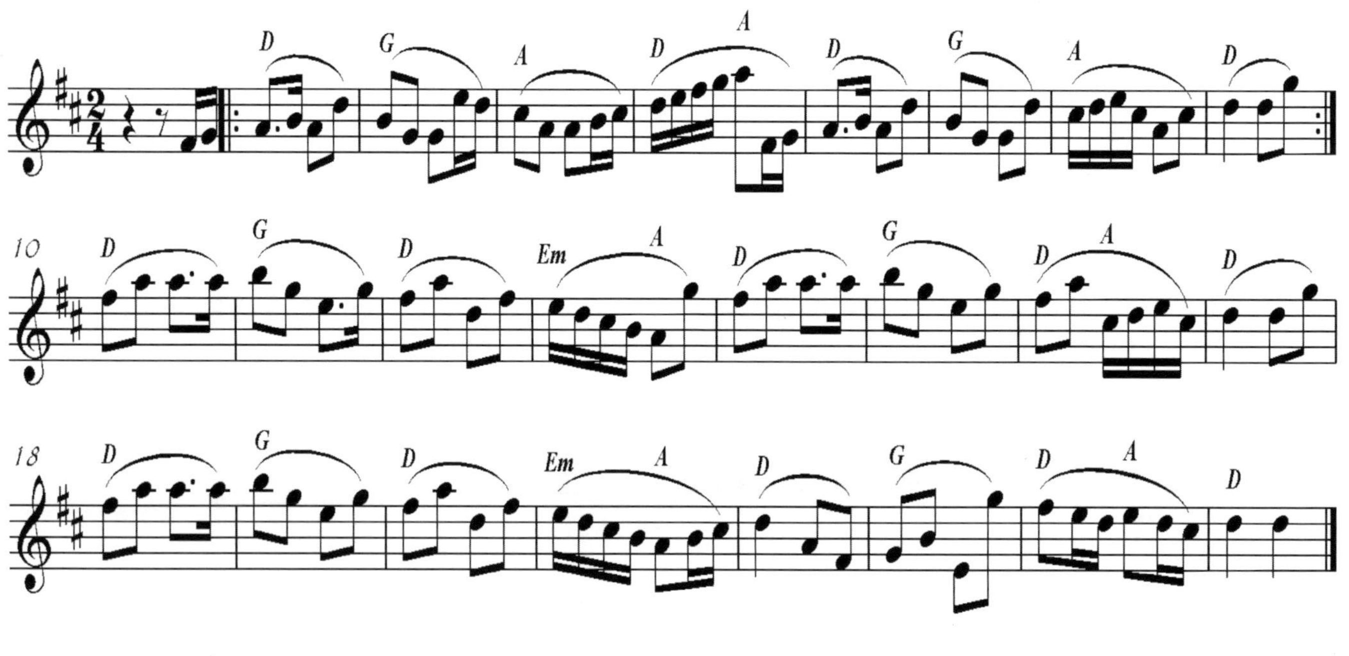

The 72nd Highlander's Farewell to Edinburgh

Traditional

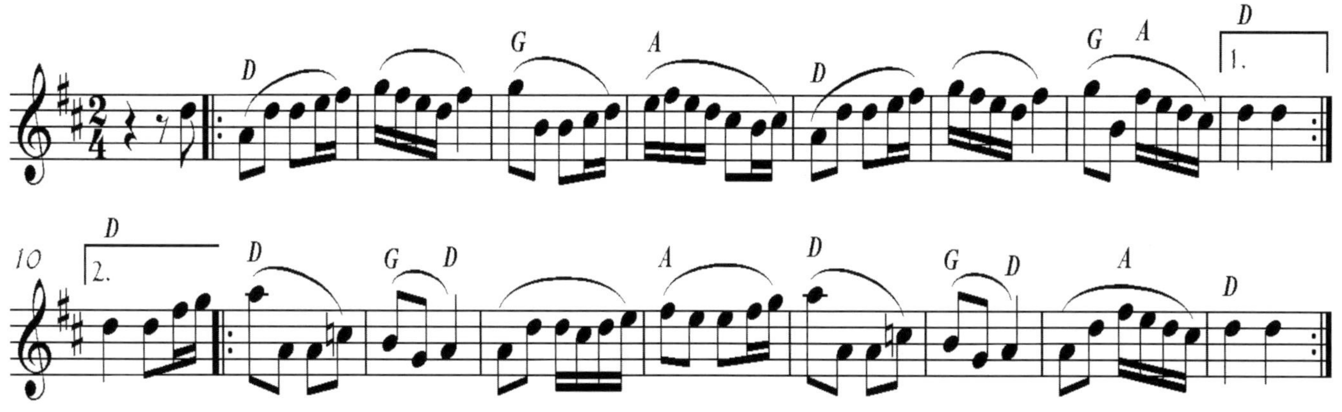

Standard Guitar Chords

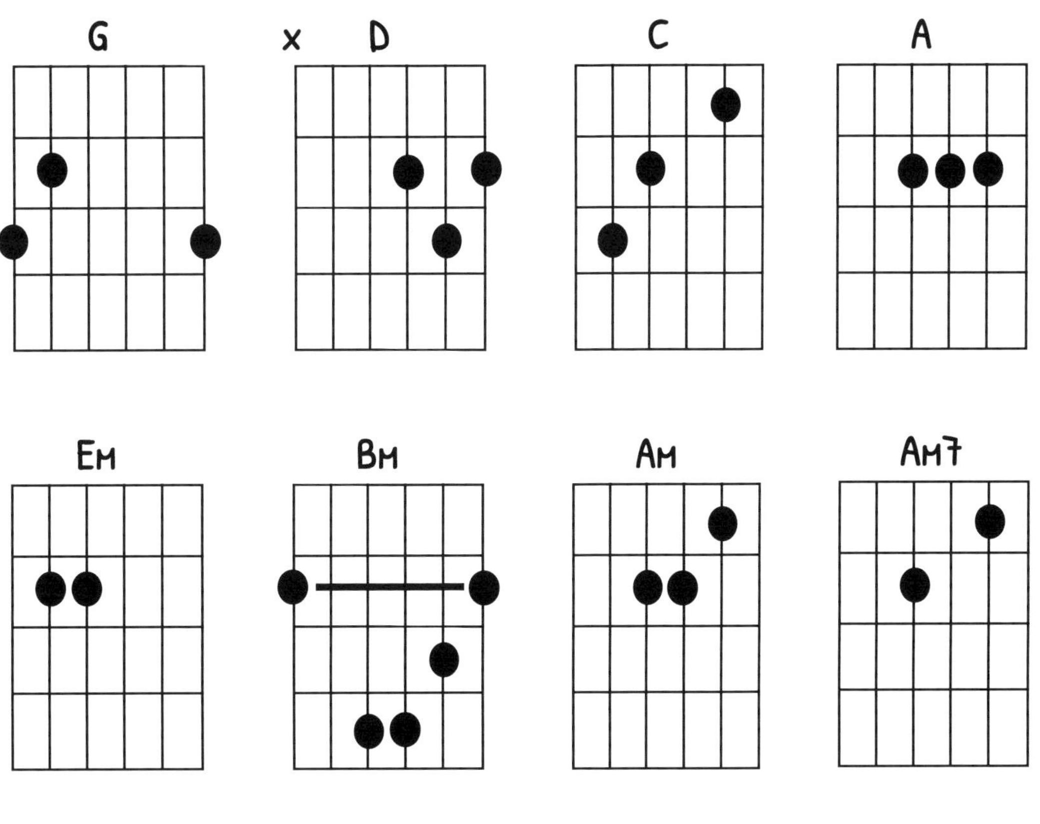

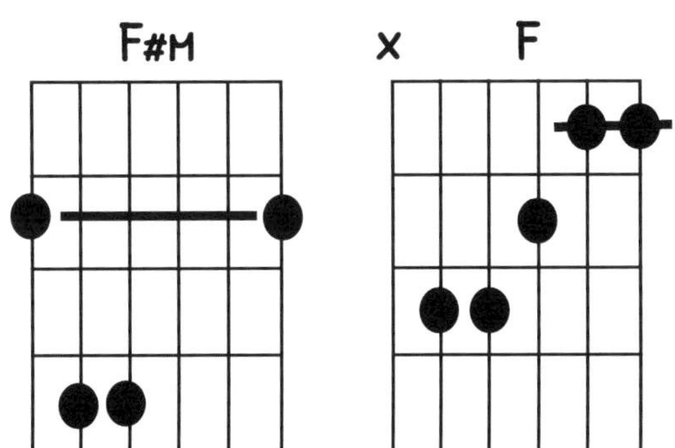

Open – D Guitar Chords – D A D F# A D

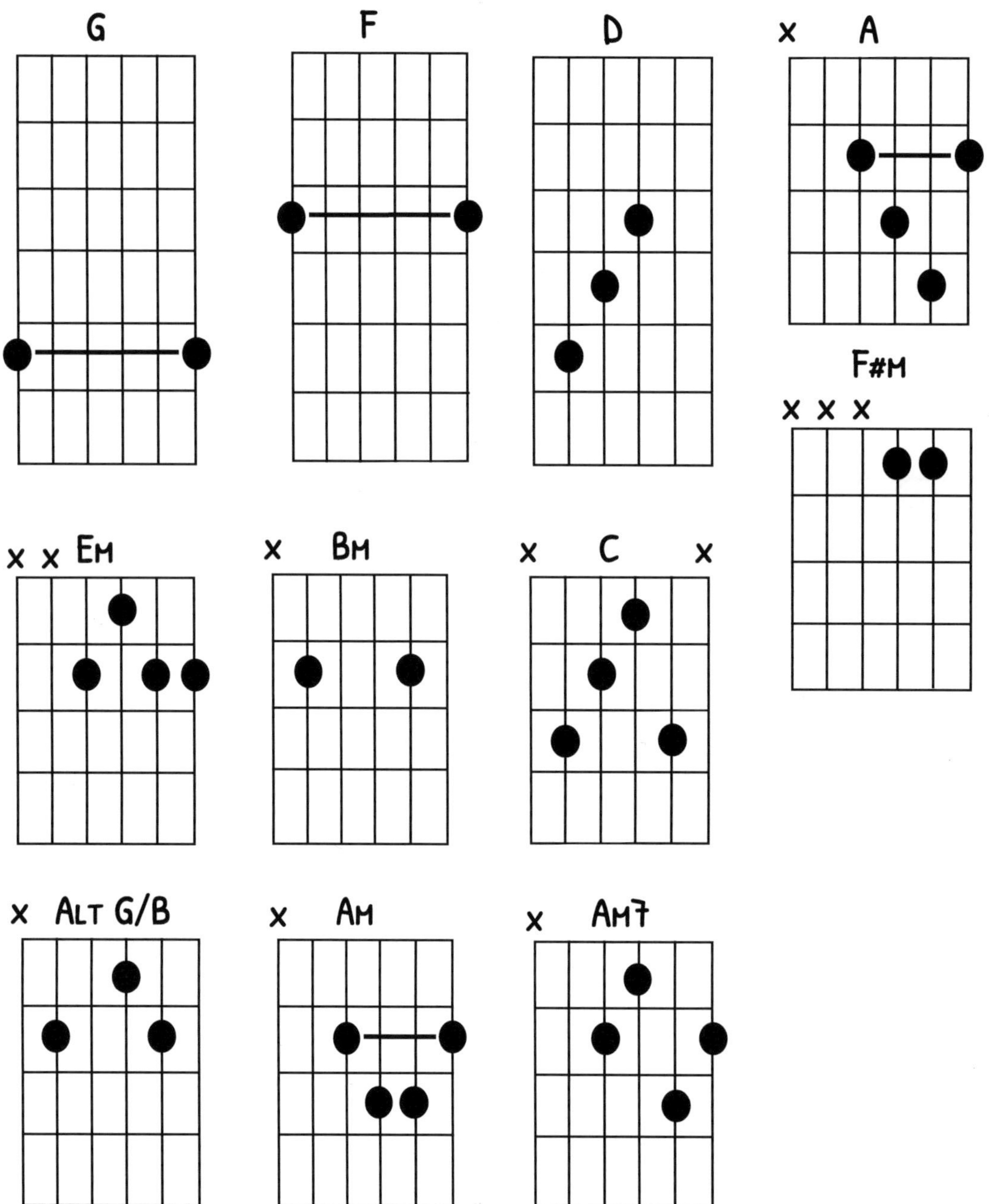

Notes for Musicians;

The tune sets for each dance don't need to be set in stone. They can be swapped around in several ways. For example, the music for the Canadian Barn Dance can also be used for the Highland Scottishe, just bear in mind the different accent and speed of the tunes to fit the dance. Likewise, the music for the Brittania Two-Step can also be used for the Boston Two-Step and the Eva 3-Step. The reels can also be swapped around between The Dashing White Sergeant, the Virginia Reel, Circassian Circle and the Cumberland Square Eight, etc. and the same can be said for the waltzes so there is plenty of scope for variety in the music.

The band set up might include fiddle, accordion, drums and maybe keyboard and bass but you can also use other combinations of instruments that will work perfectly well.

The lead instruments are usually fiddle and accordion, but you can also use a piano to lead as well as the mandolin, tenor banjo and whistle or flute. You don't need a full drum kit either. A snare and bass drum will be okay or even a cajon

Enjoy your ceilidh dancing!

Kevin Allison

About the Author

Kevin Allison lives in East Kilbride, South Lanarkshire, Scotland, where he has lived most of his life.

His interest in playing traditional music started when he was fourteen years old and first learned to play the tin whistle. As his interest in music developed, he began learning other instruments, including guitar, mandolin and piano. Through the years he has also turned his hand at playing the accordion, banjo, flute and percussion.

Kevin believes he has been fortunate to have had the opportunity and experience of gigging with numerous bands and musicians over the years, mostly around Glasgow, playing at concerts, ceilidhs, sessions, and other music events .

He hopes that in writing this book, he is able to share his passion for traditional music, and especially with those who have a particular interest in Ceilidh Dancing!

Other Mel Bay Books of Interest

100 Tunes from O'Neill's Music of Ireland for Mandolin (Allison)
Renaissance Tunebook (Holenko)
Contra Dance Encyclopedia (Holenko)
300 Gems of Irish Music for All Instruments (Larsen)
A Dossan of Heather/Irish Music of Donegal (Byrne/Jones/Duval)
Acoustic Music Source Book (Matteson)
Bluegrass Picker's Tunebook (Matteson)
Cantiga's Renaissance Festival Favorites (Bielefeld)
Irish Session Tunebook (Fuchs)
Klezmer Collection: C Instruments (Phillips)
Ryan's Mammoth Collection of Fiddle Tunes (Sky)
O'Neill's Music of Ireland (Complete Edition)
Forget Me Not (Seamus Connolly/L. Martin)
Irish Fiddle Music from Counties Cork and Kerry (Beisswenger/O'Connell)
Dance ce soir: Fiddle and Accordion Music of Quebec (Hart/Sandell)
Fiddle Music of Prince Edward Island (Perlman)
Anthology of Contest Fiddle Tunes (Carr)
The Phillip's Collection of Traditional American Fiddle Tunes Vol. 1
Ozarks Fiddle Music (Beisswenger/McCann)
Old-Time Festival Tunes for Fiddle & Mandolin (Levenson)
Favorite American Waltzes for Fiddle (Phillips)
Favorite American Polkas and Jigs for Fiddle (Phillips)
Kenny Hall's Music Book: Old-Time Music for Fiddle & Mandolin
Uff Da! Let's Dance: Scandanavian Dance Tunes/Mandolin (Bruce)
Uff Da! Let's Dance: Scandanavian Dance Tunes/Accordion (Bollerud)
Parking Lot Picker's Songbook/Fiddle (Bruce/G. Jones)
Parking Lot Picker's Songbook/Mandolin (Bruce)

WWW.MELBAY.COM

EXCELLENCE IN MUSIC
MEL BAY®
Since 1947